Abraham Lincoln

Published by Roaring Brook Press
Roaring Brook Press is a division of Holtzbrinck Publishing Holdings Limited Partnership
175 Fifth Avenue, New York, NY 10010
mackids.com

Library of Congress Control Number: 2017957496
ISBN 978-1-250-16611-1

Our books may be purchased in bulk for promotional, educational, or business use. Please contact
your local bookseller or the Macmillan Corporate and Premium Sales Department at (800) 221-7945
ext. 5442 or by e-mail at MacmillanSpecialMarkets@macmillan.com.

First published in France in 2016 by Quelle Histoire, Paris
First U.S. edition, 2018

Text: Albin Quéru, Romain Jubert
Translation: Catherine Nolan
Illustrations: Bruno Wennagel, Mathieu Ferret

Printed in China by RR Donnelley Asia Printing Solutions Ltd., Dongguan City, Guangdong Province
10 9 8 7 6 5 4 3 2 1

Abraham Lincoln

Roaring Brook Press
New York

A Difficult Start

Abraham Lincoln was born on February 12, 1809, in Kentucky. His family called him Abe.

Abe's parents were farmers. His sister was two years older. They all lived in a one-room log cabin. Times were tough, and sometimes they didn't have enough food.

From a young age, Abe worked hard to help his family. Then his mom became very sick.

—

1809–1816

A Curious Child

Abe's mother died when he was only nine years old. A year later, his father married a widow named Sarah Johnston.

Abe liked his stepmother. She encouraged him to read and write. She would travel dozens of miles to find him new books. Young Abe loved to read. He was interested in everything.

———

1818–1819

Adventure

Abe stayed curious as he grew up. He tried many different jobs. When he was twenty-one, he worked on a flatboat. He led a trip down the Mississippi River to New Orleans.

Then he took a job in Illinois, helping out a lawyer. He learned all about the law and became a lawyer himself.

———

1830–1831

First Steps in Politics

Next Abe tried politics. He ran for Congress and won! Abe moved to Washington, DC. He was excited to serve his country. He talked about an issue that was very important to him: slavery.

At that time in America, white people could own black people as slaves. Abe knew it was wrong, so he spoke out against it. Another politician, Jefferson Davis, spoke in favor of it.

Abe and Jefferson became rivals.

———

1846

A Step Back

Abe lost his next election. He went back to Illinois and to his job as a lawyer.

Years passed. People far and wide praised Abe. They said he was a fine lawyer. A fine man, too—honest and smart.

Friends told Abe he should try politics again. Abe decided to do it. Only this time, he ran for president!

———

1848–1859

Advice

Abe took a trip across the country, making speeches. He hoped the people who heard him speak would vote for him.

During his trip, Abe got a letter from a young girl named Grace Bedell. Grace told Abe to grow a beard. She said it would bring him luck.

Abe listened to Grace. Just days after winning the election . . . he grew a beard!

———

1859–1860

President Lincoln

On March 4, 1861, Abraham Lincoln became the sixteenth president of the United States.

It was a hard time to be president. The whole country was fighting about slavery.

States in the North agreed with Abe. They wanted to outlaw slavery. States in the South agreed with Abe's old rival, Jefferson Davis. They wanted slavery to remain.

War broke out between the North and the South.

———

1861

The American Civil War

The soldiers from the North wore blue uniforms. They were called Union troops, or Yankees.

The soldiers from the South wore gray uniforms. They were called Confederate troops, or Rebels.

The war lasted four terrible years. More than 620,000 soldiers died. In the end, the Yankees outfought the Rebels. The North won.

1861–1865

Guiding America

Abe led the country well during the war.

In 1863, he signed a document that declared millions of slaves were freed. It was one of his greatest acts as president.

In 1863, he established a national holiday. From then on, Thanksgiving would be held on the last Thursday in November.

As the war ended, he urged both sides to make peace. Abe wanted America to be strong again.

———

1863–1865

Good-bye

Some people from the South would not make peace. They were angry that their side lost the war. One of them was John Wilkes Booth.

Five days after the war ended, Abe went to a play with his wife and some friends. John Wilkes Booth sneaked a gun into the theater. He shot the president.

Abraham Lincoln died the next morning, April 15, 1865. To this day, he is one of America's most admired presidents.

—

April 14–15, 1865

1809
Abraham Lincoln is born.

1819
Abe's father, Thomas, marries Sarah Johnston.

1834
Abe starts studying law.

1842
Abe marries Mary Todd.

1800

1818
Abe's mother, Nancy, dies.

1830
Abe works as a flatboat guide.

1837
Abe gives his first speech against slavery.

1847
Abe moves to Washington, D

1851
Abe's father dies.

1861
Abe becomes president.

1862
Confederate soldiers win a big battle in Fredericksburg, Virginia.

1865
Slavery is officially outlawed in the United States.

1865
Abraham is assassinated.

1870

1860
Abe wins the presidential election.

1861
Start of the Civil War.

1863
Union soldiers win a big battle in Gettysburg, Pennsylvania.

1865
End of the Civil War.

The Civil War

MAP KEY

1 Hardin County, Kentucky

Abraham Lincoln was born in this county in Kentucky. The Lincoln family lived in a small log cabin.

2 Washington, DC

This is the capital of the United States. Abe lived here when he served in Congress and again when he was president.

3 New Orleans, Louisiana

Abe guided a boat to this southern city at the mouth of the Mississippi River in 1830. He saw how terrible slavery was during this trip.

4 Battle of Fort Sumter, South Carolina

The first battle of the Civil War was fought in Charleston Bay, South Carolina. Confederate troops took Fort Sumter from the Union troops.

5 Battle of Fredericksburg, Virginia

The Rebel army won this battle in Fredericksburg, Virginia, on December 13, 1862.

6 Battle of Antietam, Maryland

Twenty-three thousand soldiers were killed, wounded, or went missing during this battle near Sharpsburg, Maryland. The Union side won.

 Confederacy   **Union**

People to Know

Sarah Johnston
(1788–1869)
She was a widow with two daughters and a son. She married Thomas Lincoln, Abe's father.

Ulysses S. Grant
(1822–1885)
Abe named him commanding general of the Union army. Later, he was twice elected president of the United States.

Robert E. Lee
(1807–1870)
He was an officer in the U.S. Army until 1861,
when he left to become a Confederate general.
He surrendered to Grant in 1865.

Jefferson F. Davis
(1808–1889)
He was Abe's rival for many years.
Jefferson was president of the Confederate
states from 1861 to 1865.

Abe was the first president with a full beard! At six feet four inches, he was the tallest president, too.

Abe invented a device to lift riverboats over sandbanks. He's the only U.S. president so far to have a patent registered in his name.

Abe was a skilled wrestler.
In 1992, he was added to the
National Wrestling Hall of Fame.

Abe didn't go to college or law
school, yet he became a successful
lawyer. He learned about the law
from reading books and working
for other lawyers.

Available Now

 Muhammad Ali

 Neil Armstrong

 Blackbeard

 Coco Chanel

 Charlie Chaplin

 Cleopatra

 Marie Curie

 Albert Einstein

 Abraham Lincoln

 Nelson Mandela

 Isaac Newton

 Rosa Parks

Coming Soon

 Anne Frank

 Gandhi

 Frida Kahlo

 Martin Luther King, Jr.